The Bullying Phenomenon

BREAKING THE CYCLE

DWAYNE RUFFIN, ED.D

WestBow
PRESS®
A DIVISION OF THOMAS NELSON
& ZONDERVAN

WestBow Press books may be ordered through booksellers or by contacting:

WestBow Press
A Division of Thomas Nelson & Zondervan
1663 Liberty Drive
Bloomington, IN 47403
www.westbowpress.com
1 (866) 928-1240

ISBN: 978-1-5127-7348-4 (sc)
ISBN: 978-1-5127-7349-1 (hc)
ISBN: 978-1-5127-7347-7 (e)

Library of Congress Control Number: 2017901313

Print information available on the last page.

WestBow Press rev. date: 02/15/2017

DEDICATION

This book is dedicated to my ancestors past, and present in whom I stand today in their fervor, prayers, and conviction. To my wife Tiffany, my children, and my parents for their sacrifice, love and support. To fellow educators in whom we stand together on the front line eradicating illiteracy and encouraging life long learners. Lastly, to my armed service comrades who defend this nation's civil liberties without regard to unimaginable sacrifice.

CONTENTS

Introduction ix

Chapter 1 1

Chapter 2 9

Chapter 3 13

Chapter 4 17

Chapter 5 31

Chapter 6 35

Chapter 7 71

References 75

Additional Resources 99

About the Author 101

INTRODUCTION

> To move forward, there must be a sustained effort
> to listen to each other; to learn from each other: to
> respect one another; and to seek common ground.
>
> —Barack Obama

The Bullying Phenomenon is a concise guidebook and literature review that focuses on a veritable epidemic of bullying that is affecting students in both middle school and high school. Surveying pertinent literature and studies on bullying and offering correctives to help confront the problem of bullying and its lasting effects, the author invites readers to take up the cause to intervene in bullying and do what they can to work with community and school leaders to prevent it. The notion of Breaking the Cycle draw attention to interventions (The Bullying Resolution Model, Anti-bullying legislation, Gentle in tolerance, Proactive anti-bullying posture, Mediation, Developmental training, Conflict De escalation strategies and Restorative practices) that contest the Bullying Phenomenon. Consequently, the bullying model components can address multi-level conflicts ranging from minor inappropriateness to sever or even complex dilemmas.

CHAPTER 1

Peace is not absence of conflict, it is the ability to
handle conflict by peaceful [restorative] means.

—Ronald Reagan

Introduction

Student bullying exists as an egregious, insidious, and antisocial behavior that traumatizes millions of students each year. Pintado (2006) suggested that bullying is a common occurrence in schools. Additionally, student bullying is exacerbated by school faculty and parents who lack awareness and do not create interventions for the prevalence of bullying that exists in the school climate. However,

Feinberg (2003) and Hellams (2008) placed less emphasis on the significance of student bullying.

Feinberg (2003) and Urbanski (2007) also suggested that bullying was historically dismissed as an ordinary part of child development. For example, the evolution of boys into manhood or masculinity consists of rough-and-tumble play that frequently occurs as wrestling, climbing trees, jumping over fences, and playing with soldiers through toys and video games that kill the enemy through hand-to-hand combat or even with weapons of mass destruction.

In addition, the growth of adolescent girls into femininity consists of being more verbal in speaking their minds. This pattern also involves forming groups or cliques that generally consist of four to five friends who share a common interest. The significance of *The Bullying Phenomenon* is that it can serve as a catalyst in breaking the bullying cycle among our youth, first through raising awareness and, second, through taking actions that results in conflict resolution (the bullying resolution model).

The Bullying Phenomenon: Breaking the Cycle has been written as a way to contend with the prevalence of student bullying; the author also hopes to instigate change in dealing with issues of bullying. *The Bullying Phenomenon* recommends that readers of the book include but not be limited to legislators, school leaders, teachers, parents, school paraprofessionals, community and mental health agencies, and concerned citizens who desire to anticipate and intervene in bullying activities that may hinder effective academic progress in a school or threaten the safety of a school climate.

The Bullying Phenomenon also provides educational practitioners with information that informs their recommendations for designing action plans that may provide valuable information to validate appropriate student safety plans, bullying prevention programs, teacher professional development, parent conferences, or even the review of antibullying legislation.

Bullying Scenarios

Cornish suggests that using scenarios as a projection analysis is an excellent predictor of conflict (bullying) occurrences within a given organization's environment; Cornish also suggests that this aids the leadership in assessing or anticipating future climate trends.

First Scenario

Lydia is a very popular and active student in school. She is in the tenth grade and maintains a 3.0 GPA; she is also captain of the school's dance team. Lydia and her friends were caught harassing another team member who is less popular, unattractive, and lacks dancing skills in comparison to the other team members. On one particular occasion, Lydia was overheard talking about the team member, saying how ugly she was. As the team member approached the group, Lydia proceeded to exclude her from the group by encouraging the other girls to walk away once the young lady approached.

Bully's response: When the teacher confronted the girls involved, they replied, "We were just having fun and joking around, weren't we?" The victim responded with a yes, and her face contorted into one of apparent disgust and annoyance.

Second Scenario

Brice has been at his school since preschool, but now he is in the seventh grade. The perception of Brice by others has been negative because of his history of fighting, being disruptive in class, and talking back to the teacher. Although Brice's behavior has improved, he is still viewed as a bully. On a day during the regular teacher's absence, Brice was walking to his seat when another classmate stuck his foot out, causing Brice to trip and fall. At the time, the substitute teacher's back was turned, and therefore the substitute did not witness the victimization. Brice immediately responded, and his first reaction was pushing the student back.

Comment: This particular incident highlights the rituals of bullying and how roles change depending on the situation. Although Brice's behavior usually identifies him as a bully, within this scenario he was the victim.

Third Scenario

Donald is in the eighth grade. He is much smaller than his other peers, including the girls. Donald is also quiet, and he tries hard to make friends by giving them gifts. Donald has been getting pushed around and teased since the beginning of the year, and he doesn't tell anyone, because he thinks that he would lose what he considers to be his friends. In January, another boy said Donald was walking too slowly as they were going to lunch, so the boy pushed him down.

Bully's response: The incident was immediately investigated by the school administration, and it included witnesses for both boys along with due process rights and parent contact. However, Donald (the victim) tried to justify the incident by saying, "We were just playing" (as if playing within the school's confines is not inappropriate).

The significance of these scenarios highlights how bullies verbally dodge taking ownership for their inappropriate action during school investigations of misconduct. Consequently, the bullies' abilities to maneuver around implicating investigations should be considered, particularly since students are frequently reluctant to report bullying behaviors to school administration, teachers, and parents for fear that nothing will be done or that it will make the situation worse. This is the victim's reality.

We have a powerful potential in our youth, and we must have the courage to change old ideas and practices so that we may direct their power toward good ends.

—Mary McLeod Bethune

Background

Although bullying has been widely investigated in the last decade, it appears that adults are aware of only a small amount of the bullying behavior found in schools. Bullying is a widespread problem that has its greatest influence and prevalence during middle school and high school years. Bullying is a covert ritual that often goes undetected because bullying in schools is considered low-level violence; however, it is the most prevalent form of low-level violence in schools today. One third of US students experience bullying either as a target or as a perpetrator, which has resulted in the highest increase of student bullying among America's students between grades six through twelve.

Case in point: Thirty-two students were killed in Virginia; twenty-three were killed and thirty-two wounded at Thurston High; and recently a mob of teenagers beat Darien Albert to death—a sixteen-year-old honor student who attended Fenger Public High School in Chicago. Although bullying is not as overt as weapons offenses and fatal shootings, it occurs with greater frequency and may have a profound and lasting effect on student mental health, social relationships, and school performance. Student bullying is further exacerbated by the fact that school faculty stakeholders frequently do not recognize the extent of bullying in their school setting. Therefore the empathy and compassion of a teacher about a bullying incident does not always lead to intervention. In fact, collective research studies have consistently indicated that teachers intercept only a small percentage of bullying challenges.

This is especially the case when bullying was dismissed as an ordinary part of child development (Cottello 2008; Feinberg 2003). Espelage and Swearer (2011) documented elements implicated in the development and maintenance of bullying that include (a) the perceptions and actions of teachers and other adults at school, (b) the physical characteristics of the school grounds, (c) family factors, (d) cultural characteristics, and (e) community factors.

Case studies show that over a decade an estimated 75 percent of all adolescents in the United States had reported being bullied at school. A review of past case studies has indicated that bullying has become a well-known problem and a common occurrence in many schools throughout the United States as well as in other countries. Previous research merely identified bullying as a problem without defining the root causes of the problem or exploring the dimensions that pose a challenge in attempting to help victims and stop bullying victimization—dimensions such as covert, direct, or hard-to-detect bullying practices.

CHAPTER 2

Not everyone has been a bully or the victim of bullies, but everyone has seen bullying, and seeing it, has responded to it by joining in or objecting, by laughing or keeping silent, by feeling disgusted or feeling interested.

—Octavia E. Butler

The Nature of Bullying

The act of bullying involves physical intimidation, humiliation, and/or verbal abuse marked by victimization; it can occur over a frequency of days, weeks, or more, and it often occurs over at least six months. The roots of bullying behavior are mainly violent in nature, and some people who dominate others (or want to dominate others) have underlying social, emotional, and even physical issues urging them to control others so that their own inadequacies will not become exposed.

This is an indirect way to make the bully feel better. By degrading the victim with verbal, physical, and emotional abuse, the bully somehow eases his or her own pain, though temporarily and superficially. Consequently, the bully attempts to elevate his or her own ego through the degradation of others. This domineering and sometimes sadistic behavior seems to be genetically predisposed, but ultimately it develops from harsh parenting styles. Studies show that victims of bullying are at high risk for low self-esteem, depression, and suicide.

As an aggressive behavior, the outcome, intention, or goal of bullying is often to cause physical, emotional, or relational harm; bullying also exists in relationships where there is an imbalance of power. And lastly, bullying often occurs repeatedly over time. Research also suggests that bullying typically occurs in the presence of peers who can adopt a variety of roles, such as remaining neutral during a bullying incident, assisting and encouraging the bully, aiding or consoling the victim, or even reversing roles by assuming the position of the bully, victim, or bystander.

Victims are bullied and harassed because they are often viewed as being different. These differences may include obesity, being small in physical stature, or having learning or physical disabilities; students with different sexual orientations as well as emotional deficiencies can also be victimized often by bullying. Approximately 24 percent of students have reported participating in bullying activities; many also conveyed they had been bullied by others. In order to correct the problem, the solutions have to address the causes. The list below identifies causes of why students engage in bullying rituals.

a) lack of appreciation for diversity/uniqueness
b) need for power over peers
c) negative perceptions
d) self-image
e) beliefs
f) learning frustration
g) family instability
h) lack of classroom productivity
i) violation of personal boundaries
j) negative attitude
k) avoidance of active listening
l) identity crisis
m) lack of coherent expression of thoughts, ideas, or feelings
n) intrinsic values
o) lack of social and emotional competency and interactions
p) lack of ownership and acceptance of accountability and responsibility
q) negative or hurtful memories

CHAPTER 3

The common mistake that bullies make is assuming that because someone is nice that he or she is weak. Those traits have nothing to do with each other. In fact, it takes considerable strength and character to be a good person.

—Mary Elizabeth Williams

Types of Bullying

Bullying victimization can happen anywhere. This section provides facts on the types of bullying and also character traits of those who bully others.

1) Student victimizes others without justification.

2) Student becomes frequently violent.

3) Student has anger management issues.

4) Student manipulates and controls others and situations.

5) Student never takes ownership or responsibility for actions.

Student bullying usually involves peers who adopt a variety of interchanging roles depending on the contingency situation, such as remaining neutral during a bullying incident or assisting and encouraging the bully in victimizing their prey, aiding or consoling the victim, or even reversing roles by assuming the position of the bully, the victim, or the bystander.

Physical bullying is a term referring to bullying activities that include hitting, pushing, punching, and kicking others. Physical bullying can include harassment like name calling or stalking behaviors, and more violent abuses like hitting or intimidating. Sometimes groups of young adults target and alienate a peer because of an adolescent prejudice. This can quickly lead to a situation where he or she is being taunted, tortured, and beaten up by fellow classmates. Physical bullying can end tragically and therefore must be stopped immediately.

Relational bullying activities results in name calling, threatening behavior, teasing, dirty gestures, or mistreatment of others by ignoring and excluding them from a group or spreading rumors, as well as making or writing degrading comments about a person, deliberately excluding him or her from activities, not talking to a person, or damaging the belongings of others.

Relational bullying is most prevalent among girls in grades five to eight. Female bullies are often popular and charismatic girls who are praised by adults and rarely suspected as bullies. These girls use relational bullying typically as a way to decrease the victim's social status as they increase their own. Relational bullies use the normal human need for belonging, acceptance, and friendship against their victims, using the power of the group as a tool to harm or control their victims. Relational bullies intentionally manipulate and damage the relationships of their victims as a means to gain or maintain power.

Emotional bullying refers to the negative activities in which a person is made to feel isolated and ridiculed largely through mechanism such as teasing, shouting, mocking, and ignoring. This is a case where the bullying does not necessarily have a physical component and for that reason is sometimes harder to spot or rectify. Emotional bullying happens among adults and children and at locations in our society such as school and the workplace. Like other forms of bullying, there is usually no rhyme or reason as to what makes somebody a victim other than the random choice of the bully, who wants to dominate others.

Emotional bullies tend to locate victims and then set out to make them feel small and unwanted. Bullies tend to embarrass their victims within social settings and misrepresent the victim to other people as a means to gain power or popularity at others' expense. Bullies may do things to provoke anger and fear in their victims and may resort to lying and cheating to reach their goals. There are sometimes racial and sexual components to emotional bullying, such as same-sex harassment. In fact, this type of abuse leaves the victim feeling different, uncertain, and confused about his or her sexual orientation, which can have long-term repercussions, with the victim having to deal with low self-esteem and a diminished sense of self-worth.

Cyberbullying any inappropriate behavior that includes acts of bullying and aggression through electronic devices and technology intended to upset someone purposely by sending or posting malicious messages and pictures about the victim online.

Cyberbullying has propelled school violence to another level through new technologies, including computers and mobile phones used for (a) verbal insults; (b) name calling; (c) rumors; and (d) the sharing of private communication, pictures, or videos. The bully often uses the Internet and other electronic devices and social media to spread the message of physical, relational, and emotional victimization. Research indicates that approximately one third of cyberbullying victims are threatened or embarrassed each year because of information or pictures posted on the Internet about them by others.

CHAPTER 4

The man who gets the most satisfactory results is not
always the man with the most brilliant single mind,
but rather the man who can best coordinate the brains
and talents of his associates.

—W. Alton Jones

Bullying Case Studies

The following case studies were reviewed as part of an ethnographic
research project on elementary, middle, and high school bullying. The
ethnographic research design served as a data-collection medium
that allowed researchers a comprehensive means to capture data
and then describe, analyze, and interpret information related to the

bullying phenomenon. Through the ethnographic research design, data was captured that highlighted student, parent, and teacher experiences, perceptions, and emotions related to the shared essence accounts of bullying rituals. The case studies reflect the belief that incidents of bullying activities usually peak in late childhood or early adolescence. Feinberg (2003) found that most bullying victims do not feel completely safe in school and are victimized continually over a prolonged period of time.

Case 1: Global Bullying Phenomenon

Bullying is not just a United States problem; it's a global phenomenon that has emerged as a social epidemic in destroying the fabric of quality learning institutions. The demographic ages of elementary, middle, and high school students involved in bullying slightly differ in European countries from those in the United States. However, regardless of country, a common thread exists, indicating that those who are exposed to violence on both continents often suffer long-term problems such as anxiety, depression, post-traumatic stress, low self-esteem, and self-destructive behavior.

According to Harlin (2008), the data on bullying in European countries reflect increases in student bullying within Italy (33 percent); Portugal (35 percent); Netherlands (16 percent); the United Kingdom (48 percent); Belgium (21 percent); Scotland (43 percent); Wales (32 percent); Germany (29 percent); and Spain (22 percent). Although Harlin focused on student bullying in European countries, the relevance of the study provides data for a global perspective and correlates the effect of the student bullying prevalent in America. Additionally, a study involving German middle school students found reports of bullying highest beginning in grades six through nine. Consequently, the positive approach to school violence is solution-driven and consists of preventive measures and systemic efforts once an awareness of bullying is acquired. Greene (2006) additionally provided an overview of both prevention and intervention measures deployed across multiple countries where the identification of bullying as a problem of great importance occurred with the increased focus on human rights.

Case 2: Perceptions of Bullying

Differences existed between adult groups regarding the perceived responsibility for the safety of students. Parents concluded that safety is the sole responsibility of the school administration. Teachers indicated it should be a collaborative responsibility of all school stakeholders, while community members suggested the sole responsibility should be on the parents in governing the behavior of their children. In addition to the study conducted by Bellflower, Ramsey (2010) investigated the perceptions of bullying while interviewing thirteen teachers in five rural middle schools.

The results of the research were organized into three categories: (a) teacher experience with student bullying, (b) intervention and professional development, and (c) participation in policy development. Ramsey concluded that there were arrays of different perceptions of bullying severity among the participants. The study participants also indicated that interventions are largely ineffective because educators could not identify bullying rituals or were unsure of ways to handle bullying occurrences.

However, Ramsey noted, the majority of participants stated that the most serious issues of bullying in the rural middle school included both the physical and relational forms. Bellflower (2010) conducted a qualitative study comparing the perceptions of bullying by groups of six middle school students, four parents, four teachers, and four learning community members.

Results of the study indicated four underlying perceptions: (a) the main causes of middle school violence include bullying, substance abuse, students at risk due to income level at poverty line, and nonnurturing home environments; (b) peer pressure and a lack of communication promotes school violence; (c) the most frequently occurring acts of school violence were fighting, arguing, teasing, and hitting; and (d) the most serious school violence in the form of fighting occurs in isolated locations, restricted areas, or at blind corners that most teachers cannot readily observe. Bellflower (2010) concluded that unless all the school stakeholders took a more collaborative and proactive approach, the issue of school violence could continue to be problematic.

Case 3: Whole-School Approach

Case studies revealed that whole-school approaches to bullying prevention were not as successful in North American schools in past decades as they are in Norway. Norwood (2008) noted, the Olweus

(1993; 1996a) research reflect dated perceptions of North American school administrators, teachers, as well as parents, noting that they are deficient in their awareness of bullying rituals and do not perceive bullying victimization as a dangerous or serious crisis, despite the trend.

The whole-school approach to bullying prevention that draws attention to the past research of Olweus is a frequently utilized approach in schools. The Olweus (1993) bullying prevention program is a comprehensive whole-school program that was one of the first to be implemented in a large-scale manner and then systematically evaluated. The program was developed and evaluated as an intervention project involving 2,500 children in forty-two schools in the city of Bergen, Norway from 1983 through 1985.

The bullying program is a multilevel, multicomponent, school-based program designed to prevent or reduce bullying. The whole-school approach creates a dynamic and proactive school culture to prevent bullying by changing tangible aspects, such as school policy and classroom management rules targeting inappropriate behaviors, as well as student attitudes. Bellflower (2010) concluded that unless all the school stakeholders adopt the whole-school approach to bullying prevention and take a more collaborative and proactive approach, the issue of school violence could continue to be problematic.

Case 4: Bullying Occurrences

Most incidents of bullying tend to occur in isolated areas of the school confines and/or areas with minimal supervision, such as playgrounds, washrooms, locker rooms, cafeterias, halls and stairways, and school buses. The case studies data collection indicated 425 discipline referrals that were recorded during the 2013-2014 academic year (table 1). The referrals consisted of 170 physical bullying episodes (40 percent) and 144 relational bullying (34 percent) for a total of 74 percent of all inappropriate and disruptive behaviors that occurred within the school.

Subsequently, the school-archived referral data were used to determine bullying frequencies, locations, and times of bullying occurrences in the school (table 1). In addition, the examination focused on identifying when bullying episodes mostly occur during the school day; occurrence-escalation periods were also identified (table 2). The examination indicated many bullying episodes occurred during lunch (31 percent) and after lunch or during recess periods (28 percent). Locations of bullying mostly occurred in the cafeteria during lunch, in washrooms when a few students were sent unsupervised, and during recess when the ratio of adults to students was minimal (table 3).

The examination of the archived referral data as related to bullying behavior type, gender, and grade level was used to answer bullying behavior types related to grade level (tables 4). The analyses suggested that (a) bullying episodes occur across all three grade levels; (b) the ritual of physical bullying in the form of pushing, hitting, and punching was dominate among male students; and (c) relational bullying in the form of verbal name-calling, spreading rumors, teasing, and ignoring or exclusion of others mostly demonstrated dominance among female students.

Table 1

Discipline Referrals –Physical and Relational Bullying

Categories	Referrals	Percent
Number of physical bullying	174	40
Number of relational bullying	144	34
Number of other inappropriate discipline behavior	111	26
Total number of discipline referrals	425	100

Note. Data represent middle school enrollment, number of reported discipline referrals, and approximate average percent of physical and relational bullying occurrences during the 2013-2014 academic year. Chronic (five or more referrals) offenders inflated the total numbers of bullying episodes.

Table 2

Archived Referral Data as Related to Bullying Time Occurrences

Time of bullying occurrence	# Bullying referrals	Percent
Before school (before morning entry)	25	8
Morning (before lunch)	47	15
Lunch	97	31
Afternoon (after lunch recess)	88	28
During/after school (dismissal)	57	18
Total number of referrals	314	100

Table 3

Archived Referral Data as Related to Bullying Occurrence Locations

Bullying locations	# Bullying referrals	Percent
Playground and recess	50	16
Washroom	75	24
Cafeteria	97	31
Hallways	69	22
Classrooms	22	8
Total number of referrals	314	100

Table 4

Archived Referral Data Indicating Physical Bullying Occurrences

Physical Bullying	Discipline referral occurrence	Percent
Hitting, punching	78	46
Pushing	73	43
Kicking	23	9
Spitting	5	2
Physical bullying total	170	100

Table 5

Archived Referral Data Indicating Relational Bullying Occurrences

Relational Bullying	Discipline referral occurrence	Percent
Verbal name-calling	45	31
Teasing	24	17
Spreading rumors	40	28
Ignoring and exclusion	3	2
Dirty gestures	32	22
Relational bullying total	144	100

Case 5: Cyberbullying

The most common methods for electronic bullying involved the use of instant messaging, group chats, and electronic mail. Importantly, close to half of the electronic bully victims reported not knowing the identity of the perpetrator. Kowalski and Limber (2007) indicated that, out of 1,915 girls and 1,852 boys in grades six through eight who attended six elementary and middle schools in the southeastern and northwestern United States, 11 percent had been bullied electronically online at least once.

Kowalski and Limber further reported that 7 percent of the students surveyed indicated that they were victims of bullies, and 4 percent had electronically bullied someone else at least once in the previous months. In addressing cyberbullying, it is critical for those involved to recognize that, although electronic communication devices are the tools of cyberbullying, they are not the cause. In one publicized incident, at least eight middle school and high school students cyberbullied multiple people by posting photos and derogatory comments online.

The pictures and comments where posted on the social networking site Instagram, which allows users to write and edit captions for photos. Immediately after learning of the student actions through concerned parents, the superintendent contacted the police, who then assigned a detective to conduct an extensive investigation. The officer working the case, with the aid of the school district superintendent, said the posts were disturbing and accused a student of self-cutting and calling another student suicidal.

If the accused students are found guilty, they could face criminal charges as well as expulsion from the school district. In support of reducing the number of cyberbullying incidences among adolescents, the researcher identified four effective preventive strategies: (a) student offenders should not have access to social networking sites; (b) school administrators and parents should take away computer and cell phone privileges of the offenders; (c) school administrators, teachers, and parents must set clear rules and enforce consequences; and (d) school officials should be allowed to impose twenty hours of community service on offender.

CHAPTER 5

We focus so much on our differences, and that is creating, I think, a lot of chaos and negativity and bullying in the world. And I think if everybody focused on what we all have in common—which is—we all want to be happy.

—Ellen DeGeneres

Effects of Bullying

The effects of bullying are well documented and include negative impacts on student development and academic achievement. Bullying, consequently, causes psychological harm as well as a lack of normative social interactions and maladaptive outcomes for children who engage in bullying. Vreeman and Carroll (2007), as well as Dake, Price, and Telljohann (2003), noted that the media attention on homicide and suicide cases may point to increases in school bullying.

Meyer-Adams and Conner (2008) suggested that bullying may not only be the precursor of unresolved bullying, but may also be the outcome of conflicts that escalate to devastating incidents, such as the suicide of Tyler Clementi, a Rutgers University freshman, and Ryan Halligan, a thirteen-year-old boy from Essex Junction, Vermont. Other examples include the shootings at Blacksburg, Virginia, and Columbine High School in Colorado.

As a consequence, bullying within the United States is now at the forefront of the American consciousness. Concerns have increased because of high-level violence resulting from representative, well-publicized school shootings occurring in various states, such as Minnesota, Missouri, Virginia, and Ohio. In fact, research over the past fifteen years shows that bullying victims and perpetrators alike are at risk for short- and long-term adjustment difficulties with peer socialization and the attainment of academic proficiency.

Field (2007) suggested that school stakeholders realize that the perception of a child involving a single bullying incident may be traumatic whether the incident is a minor tease, purposeful bumping, or vicious physical assault. Additionally, the perception of a single bullying incident may exhibit warning signs of peer victimization.

Bullying Warning Signs

a) lost or destroyed clothing, books electronics, or jewelry

b) unexplainable injuries

c) frequent headaches or stomachaches, feeling sick, or faking illness

d) changes in eating habits, such as suddenly skipping meals or binge eating

e) coming home from school hungry because of not eating lunch

f) difficulty sleeping or frequent nightmares

g) declining grades or the loss of interest in schoolwork

h) not wanting to attend school

i) the sudden loss of friends or avoidance of social situations

j) feelings of helplessness or decreased self-esteem

k) self-destructive behaviors, such as running away and self-harm

l) talking about or attempting suicide

In 2001, 14 percent of students in grade six, 7 percent of grade nine, and 2 percent of grade twelve reported that they had been bullied at school. If children are victimized over a prolonged period, they lack the normative social interactions that are critical to their healthy development and emerging relationship capacity. Children involved in bullying are at risk for a variety of mental health problems, the most common of which is depression.

Scheithauer et al. (2006) suggested that students who are bullied show an increase in substance use, aggressive impulses, and school truancy. Studies have shown that children who participate in bullying at early ages have an increased chance of becoming engaged in criminal actions later in life.

CHAPTER 6

The great aim of education not knowledge but action.

—Herbert Spencer

Bullying Interventions

When bullying emerges within the school confines, administrators and teachers contest the inappropriate behaviors with more rules and consequences and without utilizing effective interventions that get to the student's core problem or issues. It is necessary, however, that school personnel determine the causes of these undesirable behaviors and provide restorative alternative models of behavior that might diminish or eradicate bullying in school.

The research communicates why the efforts of school officials in combating bullying rarely deliver the desired effect on student behavior. Changes must be made to affect the goal of teachers so that they may identify bullying and intervene appropriately within the existing school structures. Clarifying the process provides a meaningful and relevant contribution to the classroom environment and school climate.

Intervention 1: Antibullying Legislation

Knowledge of state and federal laws and policies may be helpful to those who are concerned with stopping bullying in the school of this present study as well as in other schools. All of the states either have a specific law or policies can be found in the criminal code of a state. The US Department of Health and Human Services, Office of Adolescent Health (2013) website listed all states as having antibullying laws and policies as well as information involving the commonalities for bullying, cyberbullying, and related behaviors. The commonalities of the states laws and policies include the following:

a) definition of bullying
b) listing of forms of antisocial behavior and how to prevent these behaviors for safety and a good learning environment
c) importance of identifying expected conduct for all school-sponsored activities, such as traveling to and from the school as well as using school-owned property
d) critical involvement of parents, school employees, and administrators, and school volunteers

e) identification of a procedure for reporting bullying

f) investigation and response to all bullying incidents

g) need for a written record of all bullying incidents

h) identification of procedures for referring the perpetrator and victim for appropriate health services

i) need to maintain and regularly update policies

j) need to development a plan for notifying students, teachers, parents of bullying policies

k) provision for the state review to ensure compliance with goals of state statutes

Although there are no federal laws that specifically apply to bullying, actions related to human rights and the overlap between bullying and harassment may be addressed through various criminal codes. As an intervention, antibullying legislation underscores the importance of reducing bullying through established policies and laws. The zero-tolerance impetus component of the NCLB mandate was not only dated but also escalated widespread use of out-of-school suspensions and expulsions for lesser or low-level school violence.

In fact, after millions of suspensions and expulsions were imposed, educators nationwide began looking for ways to ensure safety while keeping students in school. Research connects suspension with dropping out or at least with a decline in academic success. The issue that needs to be resolved is that, although students need to attend school in order to learn, if they are disruptive or violent, they not only ruin their own chances at an education but also the chances of their classmates. Therefore gentle in-tolerance disciplinary methods are suggested as a means and are adequate for low-level inappropriate behavior while reducing the effects of suspensions and expulsion that impact student learning.

1) conference with parents (telephone or face-to-face)
2) conference with administration
3) immediate correction of the inappropriate behavior (communicate rules, behavior expectations)
4) time-out room in another class (not hallway)
5) withdrawal of privileges
6) allow the students mentor to intervene
7) refer student to dean or to counseling
8) refer student to school support services
9) individualized behavior chart
10) in-house suspension
11) parent shadowing
12) temporary removal from class
13) financial restitution
14) detention after school or weekend
15) restorative questioning or conferencing
16) peace circles and/or peer juries

Attempted solutions to the unresolved school-discipline dilemma have yielded state and federal policies behind millions of out-of-school suspensions and expulsions during the past two decades. Recognizing the need to reduce the prevalence of bullying, President Barack

Obama hosted the inaugural White House Conference focused on bullying prevention.

As President Obama emphasized, no children should be afraid to attend school because of bullying peer victimization. He also stressed the belief that bullying behaviors are occurring within schools as well as through the telephones and computers of children and adolescents. In response, legislation was drafted and passed as an antibullying law.

The legislation additionally established the Bullying Task Force; members of the task force later submitted recommendations to the governor and members of the general assembly for preventing and addressing bullying in schools. The antibullying bill addressed school bullying with the goal of forbidding children from making fun of others on the basis of physical appearance, socio-economic status, academic status, pregnancy, parental status, and homelessness.

Representatives of the American Educational Research Association (2013) issued a report recommending best practices and policies for elementary, middle, and high schools to address bullying. The committee members noted that bullying needs to be understood from developmental, social, and educational perspectives and from supportive lens. The report started with the importance of a comprehensive and well-understood definition as essential to identifying the causes and assessing the connectedness and relevance of research, interventions, and legislation. Equally important is to agree on behavioral descriptors in order to know how to measure frequencies of bullying occurrences.

For example, an Illinois bill addressed four primary areas involving bullying: (a) student discipline policies, (b) the prevention of behaviors that interfere with student attendance, (c) the development of curricular programs involving Internet safety, and (d) the establishment of an Illinois bullying prevention task force.

The legislation additionally defined bullying as a pervasive physical or relational act or conduct, including communications made in writing or electronically, directed toward a student or students that has or can be reasonably predicted to have the effect of one or more of the following: (a) placing the student or students in reasonable fear of harm to the student or the property of the student; (b) causing a substantially detrimental effect on the student or the physical and mental health of the student; (c) substantially interfering with the student or the academic performance of the student; or (d) substantially interfering with the ability of the student to participate in or benefit from the services, activities, or privileges provided by a school.

Intervention 2: Proactive Antibullying Posture

Simonsen et al. suggested that the nature of bullying occurrences within school settings is typically confronted from a reactive posture and not a proactive one. Compounding this problem is the lack of widely accepted training programs for teachers related to bullying intervention. When bullying emerges within the school confines, administrators and teachers contest the inappropriate behaviors with more rules and consequences.

It is necessary, however, that school personnel determine the causes of these undesirable behaviors and provide alternative models of behavior that might diminish or eradicate bullying in school. The research communicates why the efforts of school officials in combating bullying rarely deliver the desired effect on student behavior. Changes must be made to affect the goal of teachers and administration so that they may identify bullying and intervene appropriately within the existing school structures.

Clarifying the process provides a meaningful and relevant contribution to the classroom management and safe school climate. The reality of bullying prevention is that there must be a unified call that involves not only the bully, victim, and bystanders, but also students, teachers, administrators, auxiliary staff, parents, community members, law enforcement officers, and other school stakeholders.

It is important that all involved work toward a common goal of sending the important message that bullying, regardless of what kind, will not be tolerated. Research showed that misconduct referral documents are collected yet seldom analyzed or used to make informed decisions about improving a discipline issue or designing a response that reflects specific countermeasures for bullying rituals within the school.

The bullying resolutions of Allen (2010a) and Scarpaci (2006) are heavily focused upon certain practices and design, Such as the Swart and Bredekamp notion (2009), which support the collection of relevant information in order to ensure an effective investigation of events.

The implementation of the discipline referrals was meant to (a) provide teachers and administrators with anecdotal records of student misconduct, (b) inform parents in writing of the inappropriate behavior, (c) create a consistent set of student expectations for behavior, (d) outline administrative interventions and consequences for students who engage in inappropriate behavior, and (e) reinforce positive behavior and provide students with opportunities to develop appropriate behavioral socialization skills.

The bullying intervention designed by Allen, for example, suggested educative support in an effort to improve student behaviors. This resolution mechanism is comprised of four main components, including (a) a reporting referral form, (b) an intervention, (c) a follow-up process, and (d) a record of bullying occurrences. The reporting form is meant to provide guidance to adults regarding how best to deal with the bullying incident and can be submitted in script or electronic format. Bullying is a common experience for many children and adolescents.

Field (2007) believed that when schools are run effectively and each stakeholder of the school community is respected and validated for individual uniqueness and diversity, the prevalence of bullying will be reduced. Smith (2011) reported on the latest strategies for both proactive and reactive handling of bullying in the school system. The central theme of the intervention suggested the need for peer support as perhaps the best remedy for interceding in the potential harm that can result from bullying intimidation.

Smith examined the varied roles of fostering open communication to uncover feelings and sentiments involved in bullying. Smith suggested that, while contingent upon each situation marked by divergent variables, understanding the nature of bullying techniques is critical to both diffusing and remedying the act of bullying. The contextual findings suggested that referrals must be clear and concise when reporting discipline issues to serve as necessary components of bullying prevention strategies.

Freiberg, Huzinec, and Templeton (2009), for example, analyzed the use of discipline referrals. The research showed that these referrals are rarely disaggregated to provide administrators or teachers with data-driven information or instruments to assess bullying trends proactively within schools.

O'Farrell's (2010) intervention focused on the effects of participation on elementary through high school students in a mentored peer mediation program during a school year as it related to three variables: academic achievement, developmental disposition, and conflict orientation. Conflict orientation was measured using an open-response questionnaire that provided qualitative data.

Approximately three hundred upper-grade students at five high schools participated in the dispositional and conflict orientation components. Four school districts with diverse socioeconomic, demographic, and ethnic representations were included in the study. Findings indicated that mediators were likely to implement effective conflict resolution skills while other students sought peer mediators to resolve conflicts.

Prior studies have contributed to the sustainability of mentored peer mediation programs in schools by providing a clearer understanding of the interconnections among academic achievement, developmental disposition, and conflict orientation. Powell (2007) asserted that, for some children, recess is the most important reasons to attend school. Team sports, games of chase and tag, clique-bound conversations, solitary wandering and exploration, pretend and war play, and recess offer reliable access to a scarce resource of immense value in the lives of children, involving spontaneous self-direction.

Children at recess interact with their natural environment and with each other as they choose a freedom denied them at other times while at school and increasingly in their homes and neighborhood. Powell (2007) witnessed the development of an extraordinary child-centered and spontaneous world of recess play. As children entered the elementary program, their peers initiated them into a culture of fort building.

The forts, built entirely from sticks, leaves, and objects from the surrounding woods, were sites of considerable experimentation with different forms and rules of social organization and various styles of construction. The forts were also the vehicles for much of the conflict that occurred at the school. Children negotiated and clashed over ownership of land and resources and argued about the rules and roles of fort play, involving whether the rights of those already identified with a structure outweighed the rights of outsiders to be included. In doing so, students developed and influenced reasoning about such moral principles as benevolence, justice, and reciprocity.

Fort play is unpredictable, immediate, exciting, and fun. The activity serves as a brief window of opportunity, among hours of mostly adult-inspired activities and expectations, in which children are free to manage their own lives and interact with each other on their own terms. As in the case of other schools where fort play has flourished, the forts are not a programmed activity but rather a spontaneous one that simply is not stopped.

Ongoing budget cuts have caused reductions in special and physical education programs and the number of faculty members as cost-cutting measures. There is a great deal of scholarly research that indicates physical education and activity help students in the classroom and outside as well. According to representatives of the National Association for Sport and Physical Education (2006), all elementary school children should be provided with at least one daily period of recess of at least twenty minutes.

Various cited organizations support school recess as an integral component of a child's physical, social, and academic development, providing children with discretionary time to engage in physical activity that helps them develop healthy bodies and to enjoy movement. Recess also allows children the opportunity to practice life skills including cooperation, taking turns, following rules, sharing, communication, negotiation, problem solving, and conflict resolution.

Furthermore, participation in physical activity may improve attention, focus, behavior, and learning in the classroom. The school culture may influence the bullying actions many students display, and these actions are more apparent during recess or other less-structured activities. Therefore, school administrators, teachers, and parents should not tolerate any level of bullying and should enforce social norms deemed accepted and expected. Gastic and Gasiewski (2008), as well as Peterson and Skiba (2001), suggested that bullying interventions are best resolved when climate changes are made.

According to Gastic and Gasiewski, educators must create a common line of communication between the school, home, and community. This practice often allows all stakeholders to set mutual goals as they relate to bullying preventions and antibullying action plans, ensuring that antibullying policies are present in both the home and community environments. According to Allen (2010a), the bullying intervention system is designed to offer educative support in an effort to improve student behaviors.

This resolution mechanism is comprised of four main components: (a) a reporting form, (b) an intervention, (c) a follow-up process, and (d) a record of bullying occurrences. The reporting form is meant to provide guidance to adults regarding how best to deal with the bullying incident and can be submitted in a paper or electronic format. Any staff member can submit the referral form. Once the report form is received, the administrative staff members are trained by the school's social-emotional learning intervention team to incorporate an array of differing responses.

The staff member then notifies the school administrator as well as student coaches to intervene. The collaborative team creates a plan of intervention that includes environmental modifications, family conferences, and a student-support approach that emphasizes empathy, shared responsibility, and problem solving. The bullying intervention system also requires that student coaches implement weekly follow-ups with students in an effort to determine progress or implement additional strategies.

In another study on bullying, Olthof et al. (2011) investigated whether bullying is a strategic behavior primarily aimed at attaining social dominance. The researchers conducted this study among 1,129 students ages nine to twelve years from various school systems in the Netherlands. The findings of the investigation confirmed that bullying could be correlated to desires for gaining power or dominance over others through physical or relational intimidation.

The result of the study suggested that those students who are most apt to intercede in bullying activities are socially dominant yet chose not to approach the issue to protect the victim. This study supported the key role of better understanding the mental state of the bully as a precursor to successfully deploying intervention strategies proactively, an objective well supported through teacher awareness training. Olthof et al. revealed that the key to understanding the mental state of the bully is to identify intervention strategies and provide training for teachers to identify bullying behaviors.

The study also helped to explain the underlying correlation of why bullying occurs within a school. In another case study, Skrzypiec et al. (2011) surveyed 452 students, ages twelve to fourteen, in an Australian high school, in a quest to determine how students are bullied. Through the study, they also examined the subsequent coping mechanisms of students for managing the consequences of bullying.

The researchers found significant differences in how male and female students cope with bullying while identifying the use of problem-centered, emotion-centered, and avoidance behaviors for dealing with problematic behaviors. Again, there was significant indication of the need for gaining not only understanding of the root cause of the bullying behavior, but also how to talk through why such aggressive behaviors evolve among students, delineating the value of mediation as a appropriate measure to address conflict proactively in advance of the bullying act.

Holmgren et al. (2011) explored various methods intended to decrease bullying behaviors. Through the study, they explored the effects of discussing literature, role-playing, and defining bullying in accordance with a group of rules based on consensus. Of particular note and relevance to the development of this conflict manual, they highlighted the success of peer mediation strategies toward effectively dealing with the incidence of bullying across a wide array of variables, regardless of demographic factors.

Nix and Hale (2007) revealed that positive peer mediation strategies provide an amicable method for peacefully negotiating solutions to interpersonal conflicts typical to bullying. Epstein, Atkins et al. (2008) further suggested empowering students through peer mediation strategies that focus on peer juries. Peer juries are implemented under the supervision of the school administration as student courts convene to mediate bullying episodes.

Peer juries involve mock court hearings at the school. In order to appear before a school peer jury, the referred student must admit to committing the misconduct, and then the student and parent must agree to abide by the agreements made between the referred student and the school peer jury by completing the recommended disciplinary actions. The articles provide ample evidence of the need for promoting an intervention of open dialogue and bullying awareness training among learning institutions as an intervention on the rituals of student bullying.

The evidence suggested a clear delineation of appropriate steps for increasing the awareness and preventive measures in the school environment to thwart the act of bullying. Overall, research suggested that the bullying epidemic is serious within most school environments. In essence, a close analysis of the research suggested that the problem worsens each year.

Intervention 3: Bullying Resolution Model

The Bullying Resolution Model, as well as the identification of five core elements of a bully, was researched and developed by the author as an intervention medium to affect changes in low-level violence (bullying) in schools. The bullying resolution model serves as a positive approach to school violence. It is solution-driven, consisting of preventive measures as well as systemic efforts once an awareness of bullying is acquired. The targeted audience will be educators, parents, the community, and social-emotional behavior agencies.

The model can be used with K-12 students. The research-base model can empower and increase consumers' capacity to institute instructive, corrective, and restorative responses in attending to areas where expectations were violated due to inappropriate student behavior. In addition, the first consideration in resolving a bullying incident should be to determine the prevalence of bullying existence.

Hence, when determining the prevalence of bullying, it's imperative that investigators understand the five core character elements while examining the prevalence of the bully's inappropriate hostility toward others.

1) materialize without justification
2) involving imbalance of power
3) intent to hurt or harm
4) desire expressed through action
5) repeated over time

Bullying Resolution Model Description (Figure A)

Given a thorough demonstration, this model will show a comprehensive five-cycle approach that promotes conflict de-escalation, and resolution.

The model components consist of five driving forces embedded within the five bullying cycles purposefully designed to achieve a resolution.

1) Bullying Roles

2) Bullying Type

3) Collaborative Involvement

4) Instructive, Corrective, and Intervention

5) New Skill Acquisition

The model components operate on the concept of dynamic and synergistic methodology. Primarily, the Bullying Resolution model is dynamic in nature. The full energy and characteristics of its driving force vigorously produce or undergo change and development for the conflicted parties who are engaged in the process. The Bullying Resolution Model attribute is based on the premise of reaching a resolution by means of vigorous activity through acquiring social and emotional competency interaction skills.

The following social and emotional competency skills can be achieved through collaboratively implementing the vigorous activities of the bullying resolution model to facilitate students' capacity to resolve conflict issues.

1) fostering an environment of learning and growth

2) ownership and accountability for actions

3) relationship management

4) communicating more effectively

5) gaining an appreciation for diverse perspectives and opinions

6) active listening

7) understanding personal boundaries

8) self-awareness

9) positive self-discipline and self-control

10) problem solving

11) self-management

12) teamwork

13) responsible decision making

14) tolerance, coping, assertiveness skills

15) positive self-image

16) cultural awareness

Additionally, the model components operate on the notion of synergy. The synergistic feature of the model guides the facilitator through the resolution process for maximum effectiveness. Maneuvering two or more driving forces that are working together will achieve the desired resolution effects. The combined action of two or more driving forces is greater in obtaining a resolution than the sum of their individual effects or capabilities. Consequently, the bullying model five cycle components can address multilevel conflicts ranging from minor inappropriateness to severe or complex dilemmas. Giving much-needed support and interventions to the facilitator in confronting the apparent bully or bullies allows the facilitator to monitor setbacks and to progress to resolution with the conflicted parties.

BULLYING RESOLUTION MODEL

Figure A: The Bullying Resolution Model

The Bullying Resolution Model implementation will be communicated through the following writing and overlays (figures 1 to 5).

The bullying roles and the resolution component function are the initial cycle of the model. The bullying role determines which students are the bullies, the victims, and the bystanders (identifying the problem). The resolution component determines how in-depth a dialogue should be in resolving the conflict that caused the problem. Through an investigation, school officials can identify which students are in conflict, who initiated the conflict, the nature of the conflict, and the role each student assumes (define the problem).

The key is to remember that bullying has interchanging roles depending on the situation, and therefore the contingency situation posture works best in resolving conflicts of bullying. Leff et al. (2010) found that teachers intercept about 15 percent to 18 percent of bullying incidents. Additional, research suggests that bullying typically occurs in the presence of peers who can adopt a variety of roles, such as remaining neutral during a bullying incident, assisting and encouraging the bully, aiding or consoling the victim, and even reversing roles by assuming the position of the bully, victim, or bystander.

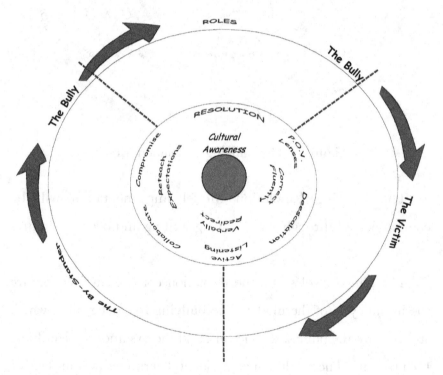

Figure 1: Bullying Roles and Resolution Stage

The next phase is bullying type. This phase functions as the second driving force of the bullying resolution cycle. Identifying the bullying type, whether it is physical, emotional, relational, or cyber in nature, aids the investigator in resolving the conflict. Clearly, this driving force identifies which medium was utilized by the offender in the victimization process (define part of the problem). Student bullying usually manifests in either one or in a combination of these forms: physical, emotional, relational, or cyberbullying.

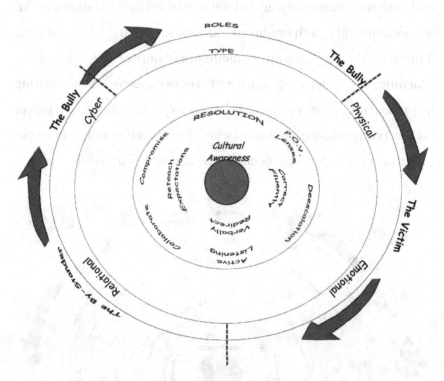

Figure 2: Bullying Roles, Resolution, Type

The collaborative involvement phase functions as the third driving force in the bully resolution cycle. The community collaborative involvement identifies the schools' learning community's internal and external resources to bring about change. For a resolution to take hold among conflicted students, they must be involved collaboratively in the problem-solving process. This consists of generating alternatives solution through collaborative dialogue and evaluating and selecting the best alternatives until a restorative posture is realized.

The developer suggests that the community collaborative involvement members consist of the school's internal community (the student, teacher, administration, parent, counselors, paraprofessionals) and external community agencies (faith-based organizations, social services, mental health organizations, and mentoring organizations). Through the collaborative facilitators illustrating, modeling, coaching, and generating conflict alternatives, as well as correlating to the learning communities, behavior expectations will empower and encourage students to make better choices, self-manage, and take ownership when conflicts occur in the absence of an adult.

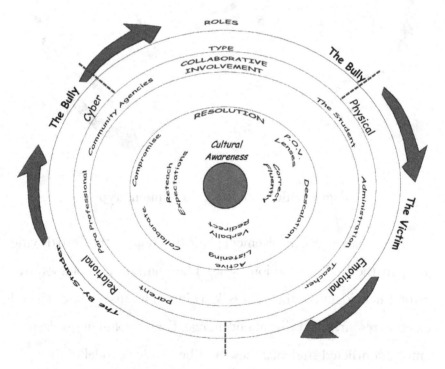

Figure 3: Roles, Resolution, Type, Collaborative Involvement

This phase focuses on instructive, corrective, and restorative responses to address the fact that misbehaviors should not lead to corporate punishments, such as suspensions and expulsion, consequences that seldom correct misbehavior or even deal with the misbehavior origin. The focus is on utilizing instructive, corrective, and restorative responses and utilizing (selecting alternatives and implementing achievable actions) nonpunitive consequence for student misbehavior (detentions, skill-building sessions, loss of privileges, and community service).

As a result, instructive responses should be used when the student's inappropriate behavior is caused by a lack of knowledge or the student does not know the desired behavior expectation. Corrective responses should be used when the student knows behavior expectations but disregards climate norms. As a behavioral response, corrective action affords the opportunity for the student to demonstrate and practice the expected behavior as a replacement for the inappropriate behavior. Restorative practice goals are to build relationships, be accountable for self and others, build social and emotional skills, and create positive solutions to repair harm.

Restorative response components include restorative questioning, peer circles, peer conferencing, and mediation. The restorative components of the bullying model focus more on harm that was caused than on the rule that was broken. Restorative questioning asks conflicted parties restorative questions such as who, when, where, why, and how in generating information relating to the incident, to choices made, and to feelings during the issue.

The construct of peer and peace circles conferencing is youth driven. These allow and encourage conflicting parties the freedom to express their viewpoints, but in a facilitated and controlled setting. For example, the goal of peace circles allows the following:

1) Students learn value and regularly use proactive, positive ways to build and maintain a peaceful classroom community.

2) Students develop and enhance positive and supportive connections with peers.

3) Students identify and learn who is affected by misbehaviors, and how.

4) Students contribute to developing appropriate ideas for how to make things right when harm has occurred.

5) Students communicate how they are affected by naming situations using affective statements and restorative questions.

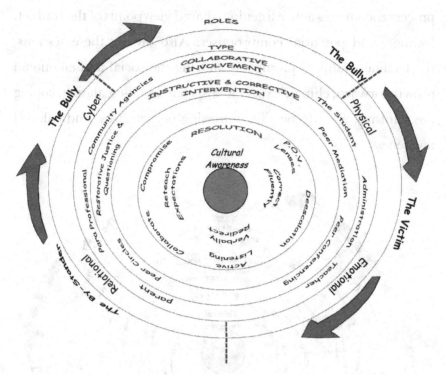

Figure 4: Bullying Roles and Resolution, Types,
Community Collaborative Involvement, and Instructive,
Corrective, and Restorative Responses

The final phase consists of the acquisition of new skills as the fifth driving force. This driving force provides opportunities for the participating parties in conflict to acquire alternative skills in dealing with issues. This process helps students take ownership and see the humanity of others. At this point, the facilitator and involved parties can sense internal emotional and mental change taking hold and beginning to effect change within the resolution outcome.

These driving forces contribute to student skill building that supports resolution outcomes. The conflicted parties are encouraged to engage collaboratively in social interaction through discussions. This process encourages active listening, shared viewpoints of the conflict, feelings, and potential compromises. Also during these sessions, the facilitator utilizes prompts in moving the social and emotional growth forward, climate expectations, conflict de-escalation, coping mechanisms, assertiveness in addressing perpetrators, and cultural awareness.

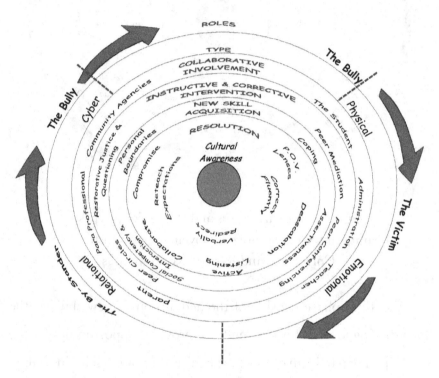

Figure 5: Bullying Roles and Resolution, Types, Community Collaborative Involvement, and Instructive, Corrective Restorative Response, and New Skills Acquisition

Intervention 4: Developmental Training

Either communications have not been clear from educational leaders or more teacher development training about bullying rituals is required. Antibullying training should include all personnel and parent volunteers who work with students on a daily basis. It is imperative for all adults interacting with children to be aware of the signs of bullying, to respond to children when they report bullying occurrences, and to support children when they are victimized after an incident.

Therefore, it is necessary for school administrators to include bullying awareness or sensitivity training to equip staff members and stakeholders with numerous antibullying strategies. To accomplish this goal, teachers must confront their own perceptions, attitudes, and misconceptions about bullying, learn skills for recognizing the indicators of bullying, and practice strategies for addressing and deterring bullying.

Research from the Center for Children and Families in the Justice System (2013) suggested that effective antibullying strategies (a) provide good supervision for children, (b) provide effective consequences for bullies, (c) provide all children opportunities to develop good interpersonal skills, and (d) create a social context that is supportive and inclusive in which bullying behavior is not tolerated by the majority.

The outcome of this intervention increases the awareness of teachers' involved in wanting to understand and identify student bullying rituals through teacher-led development training. Beaudry

(2009) suggested that greater teacher input about the topics and format of professional development activities would enhance teacher satisfaction by allowing teachers to share what they know among each other. The landscapes of academic learning institutions are forever changing and the need for relevant professional development is greater than ever. Teachers do not always feel positive about professional development activities as directed by administrators of the school district office or their school principal. Frequently, discussions among teachers during these activities reveal dissatisfaction with the existing programs. Professional development pertains to any activities intended to improve the ability of teachers to implement a new instructional program or adopt instructional techniques that will improve student performance. It is an important tool for teachers and school administrators to improve the academic or behavioral climate of a school.

Fifth Intervention: Mediation

Rosenthal (2010) conducted extensive research on a program called Learning to Live Together. This training aims to provide educators with (1) research-based "knowledge" on socio-emotional development, and on social "learning opportunities" offered by daily social and emotional events in the group setting; (2) specific intervention skills that support socio-emotional development; (3) and exploration and clarification of the overt and covert attitudes and beliefs educators may hold concerning children's socio-emotional development and concerning their own role in promoting this development. According to Shin (2010), peer mentoring helps students make connections, psychosocial and friendship characteristics of Korean children who engaged in bully/victim subgroups among their peer groups. The participants completed a peer nomination inventory as well as loneliness and social anxiety scales.

Friendship quality was measured by self-reports. Significant differences in psychosocial characteristics were found among the bully/victim subgroups, and these differences were generally consistent with those in Western cultures. Moreover, children of the same bully/victim subgroups tend to befriend each other.

Although no distinct research exists on the transformative mediation framework, it has the potential of focusing on emotions, power, and trust as well as relationship building. Unlike the traditional mediation method that forces an outcome through an authoritative approach, this method is more free-form, has no boundaries, and subtly allows disputants to own the conflict by coming up with their own solutions. The mediator owns the process and simply guides the dialogue through supportive measures.

Gunning (2004) writes, "The goals of transformative mediation are quite similar to the original goals of the community justice mediation movement insofar as both approaches take an optimistic view of parties competence and motives." Similar to Gunning (2004), who states her attraction with the transformative mediation approach, one of the writers of this paper also has an interest in this conflict-resolution framework.

Therefore, based on readings Bush and Folger (2004) *The Promise of Mediation,* a writer of this paper crafted a step-by step guide that was used as a mediation experiment by the writer in two different real work-related conflicts, both of which had the composition of workplace bullying. Disputants varied in age, gender, and length of service, which was one of the reasons for the workplace bullying relating to power.

Step-by-Step Guide Used

The writer met with each disputant separately and obtained individual assessments of the conflict. During the course of the meeting, each individual's personality and other attributes were observed. Once all assessments were completed and mentally processed by the writer, a joint meeting was scheduled. Disputants were asked to determine the place, time, and how long they felt the sessions should last. The writer used the middle point to set how long the meeting lasted. This was the initial step to get disputants to feel they were part of the process and solution. It must also be noted that school-bullying mediation must involve the parents.

Prior to meeting jointly with the disputants, the writer prepared a set of questions that were used to guide the dialogue. At the joint meeting, the writer began the session with an opening conversation that included introductions. The writer used a soft, friendly tone of voice to state a few ground rules: parties should not interrupt each other, and there should be no insults, name-calling, or blaming.

Parties were encouraged to use words, such as "When you did X, it made me feel Y," substituting what the Y was with their true feelings. Using such language is a softer way to express anger and frustration without name-calling and blaming. The writer thanked the disputants for agreeing to meet and clarified the role she would play as a mediator. The writer let the disputants know that she supported their decision making, but the decision on how they resolved the conflict must come from them and not from the mediator. Because children are involved in this school-bullying scenario, it might be helpful to use some appropriate humor to set everyone at ease and to follow a compensatory strategic approach.

The compensatory strategy approach relating to time, dialoguing, and information sharing was discussed. This approach was taken rather than a heuristic approach. Standifer, Stark, and Wall (2001) describe the compensatory strategy as allowing the flow of an extensive amount of information and time, as well as considering many alternatives and attributes.

On the opposing end, heuristic strategies involve the use of minimal information, time, and consideration of few alternatives and problem attributes. The latter approach is more appropriate when the conflict needs an immediate resolution and one has to be forced on the disputants. This should not be the case with conflicts relating to bullying, as disputing parties—parents and children alike—may need time to arrive at a decision and solve their own conflict.

The writer asked disputants to determine the order in which they wanted to speak; it was up to the disputants to determine who spoke first and last—again empowering them to make decisions. Disputants were allowed to express their true feelings without interruption and were encouraged to view the session as a conversation among team members, rather than as a mediation session whereby one person was right and the other wrong. For school-age children and their parents, the same strategy must be followed. After each disputant had made each statement, the writer reframed or restated the statement and waited for the party to either confirm or deny whether the reframing was accurate.

This was an attempt to get each speaker to reflect on his or her statement through his or her narrative, while the other parties attentively listened. The key is for the mediator to restate in the exact manner, just as the statement was originally delivered and using the same tone of voice, facial expression, or gesture as the narrator/disputant. Disputants' emotions must not be filtered out; instead, these should be encouraged without violence or unacceptable language based on the initial agreement set forth at the beginning of the dialogue.

Mediators should particularly try to explore the children's clarity or uncertainty, because sometimes children could have difficulty expressing them. All parties were allowed to reflect on the past when the conflict did not exist and reflect on how different their lives were. According to Bush and Folger (2005), reflecting on the past allows parties to gain a sense of recognition and empowerment; even children seek empowerment, as is evident in their bullying tactics.

Reflecting on the past is different from the traditional mediation model because the traditional model is concerned mostly about the present and future, and little about the past.

The writer intervened only when the situation seemed to be getting out of control. In order to come up with several alternatives for resolving the conflict, the writer introduced the disputants to a technique called brainstorming. Even children can participate in this exercise.

Brainstorming allows individuals to generate many ideas or options for consideration, and it can be a fun exercise for children as they help their parents and themselves come up with solutions. One ground rule for brainstorming is that no idea is silly; this empowers individuals to generate many solutions. Finally, the writer remained objective throughout the transformative mediation process and resisted the impulse to assist or defend.

This transformation guide worked successfully for two work-related bullying conflicts. However, adjustments must be made based on the age level of the children for the school bullying conflict. Users of this model must also be mindful that while there are many proponents of this framework, there are an equal number of opponents because the strategy lacks scholarly testing.

Sixth Intervention: Conflict De-escalation Strategies

According to the literature, there are many ways that educators and administrators can proactively prevent conflict from developing and/or escalating. Adequate staff training and school resources can provide students the opportunity to develop mutual respect themselves and others. The suggested strategies offered in the Conflict Resolution Manual focus on teaching students to manage their own behavior by allowing them to take ownership of their academics and behavior.

Strategy: Redirection/Calming (Communication), and Maintaining Proximity to Students While Teaching

Paradigm: (1) Watch for signs of student frustration that lead to misbehaviors, and utilize verbal or nonverbal cues.

(2) Quickly address misbehaviors to increase the appropriate student behaviors.

(3) Use a low tone of voice and eye contact when directing students to refocus or to stop an inappropriate behavior.

Strategy: Understanding Student Triggers That Contribute to Misbehavior

Paradigm: (1) Lack of classroom structure to include established rules. (2) Lack of preparation for changing class or transitioning to the next routine. (3) Confusing directions from the teacher on a given assignment.

Strategy: Time Management

Paradigm: (1) Create an awareness of time to help students work productively. (2) Help students to become better organized through the utilization of calendars, student planners, and assignment sheets. (3) Monitor student progress in assignments periodically.

Strategy: Giving Directions

Paradigm: (1) Face students and give directions only when you have everyone full attention. (2) Give clear, simple direction, and avoid using vague language. (3) Utilize visual aids when giving instruction.

Strategy: Environment

Paradigm: (1) Create well-organized interactive classrooms that visually stimulate students (Print Rich Environment). (2) Display classroom rules and procedures.

Strategy: Transitions

Paradigm: (1) Reduce the amount of downtime between teaching subjects. (2) Immediately engage students on entry with bell work activities. (3) Notify students of schedule changes in advance.

Strategy: Problem Solving. Analyzing the situation together with all involved parties, and integrating one's own ideas to reach a joint decision.

Paradigm: What do you think about me talking to all parties in order to find a solution?

CHAPTER 7

Summary

The dangers of bullying have escalated from the initial perception that bullying is a rite of passage that children outgrow. Hertzog (2013), the director of the National Bullying Prevention Center, stated, "The culture of bullying won't end until people across the country take action and show kids that they care." Scarpaci (2006) suggested that teachers must confront their own perceptions, attitudes, and misconceptions about bullying and learn skills for recognizing the indicators of bullying and practice strategies, as this is the most effective approach for addressing and deterring bullying.

Banks (2013) found that, although much of the research on bullying has been conducted in the Scandinavian countries, Great

Britain, and Japan, related behaviors are a force that causes negative lifelong consequences for those who bully and their victims.

Banks, who warned that bullying is a worldwide problem, believed that all students have the right to learn in a safe environment without fear. Olweus (2003) further stressed that bullying is one of the most underrated and enduring problems in school and is a reality in the lives of all students, whether they are bullies, victims, or bystanders.

Bullying has become an increasing issue in schools. Meyer-Adams and Conner (2008) suggested bullying may even be the precursor of unresolved outcomes plaguing schools such as (a) the knockout game that causes physical assault on others, (b) the suicide of countless high school and college students, or (c) school shootings throughout the United States. Criminal evidence regarding school shooters, such as Nathan Ferris, Edmar Aparecido, Brian Head, Wellington Menezes Oiverire, and Adam Lanza, indicates that 87 percent of the shooters made restoration plans for being victims of bullying.

Charmaraman et al. (2013) indicated that sexual harassment is one form of bullying. Their study examined how school staff members connect bullying and sexual harassment and their role in preventing both behaviors. The authors used four focus groups in their study with thirty-two staff members from four Midwestern public middle schools. Questions in the study were to (a) determine how many professional development opportunities for interventions are available, (b) determine the personal definitions of student behaviors as perceived by teachers, and (c) define teacher perceptions of school norms regarding bullying and sexual harassment.

The results indicated a tendency of teachers to view sexual harassment as something that occurs between adults and a lack of understanding that sexual harassment is, at times, connected with bullying. Charmaraman et al. concluded that when school administrators fail to provide professional development on both bullying and sexual harassment, staff members do not address the connection and remain unaware of policies to protect students from harmful experiences in educational settings.

The bullying referrals consisted of 170 physical bullying episodes (40 percent) and 144 relational bullying (34 percent) for a total of 74 percent of all inappropriate and disruptive behavior incidents that occurred in the study school, which had an enrollment of 533 middle school students.

Research suggests that bullying usually occurs in the presence of peers who can adopt a variety of roles, such as (a) remaining neutral during a bullying incident; (b) assisting and encouraging the bully; (c) aiding or consoling the victim; or (d) reversing roles by assuming the position as the bully, victim, or bystander.

Wang, Nansel, and Iannotti (2011), as well as Ybarra, Espelage, and Mitchell (2007), addressed Internet harassment and unwanted sexual solicitation. Ybarra et al. found that, although the majority of middle school students are infrequently involved in Internet harassment or sexual solicitation, psychological problems do result from such victimization. Consequently, educators should be aware of such acts and know effective treatments to minimize repeated behaviors.

In a related study, Lawner and Tersian (2013) studied seventeen bullying programs to determine how frequently these programs effectively changed student attitudes and practices toward bullying.

The authors found that programs involving parents are effective and that using a whole-school approach by training all teachers, administrators, and school counselors to reinforce positive behavior improves related interventions.

REFERENCES

Ali, N. M. 2010. "Enhancing transformative mediation to address family conflict." New Mexico State University. ProQuest, http://ezproxylocal.library.nova.edu/login?url=http://search.proquest.com/docview/861358914?accountid=6579.

Allen, K. P. 2010a. "A bullying intervention system: Reducing risk and creating support for aggressive students." *Preventing School Failure* 54, 199-209, http://dx.doi.org/10.1080/10459880903496289.

Allen, K. P. 2010b. "Classroom management, bullying, and teacher practices. *Professional Educator* 34(1), 1-15, http://www.theprofessionaleducator.org/.

American Educational Research Association. 2013. "Prevention of bullying in schools, colleges, and universities." Research Report and Recommendations, Washington, D.C.

Baldry, A. C., and Farrington, D. P. 2007. "Effectiveness of programs to prevent school bullying." *Victims and Offenders* 2, 183-204, http://dx.doi.org/10.1080 /15564880701263155.

Ballock, E. 2009. "What makes some learning communities so effective, and how can I support my own?" In C. J. Craig, and L. F. Deretchin, eds. *Teacher Learning in Small Group Settings: Teacher Education Yearbook XVII* (pp. 40-53). Lanham, MD: Rowman and Littlefield.

Banks, S. 2013. "Bullying in schools." Educational Resource Information Center, US Department of Education, http://www.education.com/partner/articles/eric/.

Barbetta, P. M., Norona, K. L., and Bicard, D. F. 2005. "Classroom behavior management: A dozen common mistakes and what to do instead." *Preventing School Failure* 49(3), 11-19, http://dx.doi.org/10.3200/PSFL.49.3.11-19.

Barone, F. J. 1995. "Bullying in school: It doesn't have to happen." *NASSP Bulletin* 79(569), 104-107, http://dx.doi.org/10.1177/019263659507956915.

Bauer, N. S., Lozano, P., and Rivara, F. P. 2007. "The effectiveness of the Olweus Bullying Prevention Program in public middle schools: A controlled trial." *Journal of Adolescent Health* 40, 266-74, http://dx.doi. org/10.1016/j.jadohealth.2006 .10.005.

Beaudry, K. 2009. "Improving teacher satisfaction with professional development." University of Oregon Libraries, https:// scholarsbank.uoregon.edu/xmlui/bitstream/handle/1794/10128/ ProfDevStaffMeetings.pdf?sequence.

Beavers, A. 2011. "Teachers as learners: Implications of adult education for professional development." *Journal of College Teaching and Learning* 6(7), 25-30, http://journals.cluteonline.com/index. php/TLC.

Bellflower, T. 2010. "Examining the perceptions of school violence through the views of middle school students, parents, teachers, and community members." PhD diss., ProQuest, UMI no. 3396581.

Bennett, D. 2001, "Bullying behaviors among US Youth: Prevalence and association with psychosocial adjustment." *Journal of the American Medical Association*,14(3), 32-34.

Beran, T. N. 2006. "Preparing teachers to manage school bullying: The hidden curriculum." *Journal of Educational Thought* 40, 119-28.

Biggs, B. K., et al. 2008. "Teacher adherence and its relation to teacher attitudes and student outcomes in an elementary school-based violence prevention program." *School Psychology Review* 37, 533-49.

Bowllan, N. M. 2011. "Implementation and evaluation of a comprehensive, school-wide bullying prevention program in an urban/suburban middle school." *Journal of School Health* 81, 167-73, http://dx.doi.org/10.1111/j.1746-1561.2010.00576.x.

Bradshaw, C. P., O'Brennan, L. M., and Sawyer, A. L. 2008. "Examining variation in attitudes toward aggressive retaliation and perceptions of safety among bullies, victims, and bully/victims." *Professional School Counseling* 12, 10-21, http://dx.doi.org/10.5330/PSC.n.2010-12.10.

Bradshaw, C. P., Sawyer, A. L., and O'Brennan, L. M. 2007. "Bullying and peer victimization at school: Perceptual differences between students and school staff." *School Psychology Review* 36, 361-82.

Brown, S. L., Birch, D. A., and Kancherla, V. 2005. "Bullying perspectives: Experiences, attitudes, and recommendations of 9- to 13-year-olds attending health education centers in the United States. *Journal of School Health* 75, 384-92, http://dx.doi.org/10.1111/j.1746-1561.2005.00053.x.

Bulach, C., Fulbright, J. P., and Williams, R. 2003. "Bullying behavior: What is the potential for violence at your school?" *Journal of Instructional Psychology* 30, 156-64.

Bulutlar, F., and Öz, E. Ü. 2009. "The effects of ethical climates on bullying behavior in the workplace." *Journal of Business Ethics* 86, 273-95, http://dx.doi.org/10.1007/s10551-008-9847-4.

Bush, Robert A. Baruch, and Joseph P. Folger. *The promise of mediation: The transformative approach to conflict.* John Wiley & Sons, 2004.

Carney, J. V. 2008. "Perceptions of bullying and associated trauma during adolescence." *Professional School Counseling* 11, 179-88, http://dx.doi.org/10.5330/PSC.n .2010-11.179.

Center for Children and Families in the Justice System. 2013. "Bullying: Information for parents and teachers, http://www.lfcc.on.ca/bully.htm.

Charmaraman, L., et al. 2013. "Is it bullying or sexual harassment? Knowledge, attitudes, and professional development experiences of middle school staff." *American School Health Association* 83(6), 438-44, doi:10.1111/josh.12048.

Cole, J. C., Cornell, D. G., and Sheras, P. 2006. "Identification of school bullies by survey methods." *Professional School Counseling* 9, 305-313.

Cook, C. R., et al. 2010. "Predictors of bullying and victimization in childhood and adolescence: A meta-analytic investigation." *School Psychology Quarterly* 25, 65-83. doi:10.1037/a0020149.

Cottello, J. M. 2008. "Bullying in schools: Identification, prevention, and intervention." Master's thesis, WorldCat, OCLO no. 299755599).

Craig, W. M., Pepler, D., and Atlas, R. 2000. "Observations of bullying in the playground and in the classroom." *School Psychology International* 21, 22-36, http://dx.doi.org/10.1177/0143034300211002.

Craig, W. M., and Pepler, D. J. 2007. "Understanding bullying: From research to practice." *Canadian Psychology* 48, 86-93, http://dx.doi.org/10.1037/cp2007010.

Crothers, L. M., Kolbert, J. B., and Barker, W. F. 2006. "Middle school students' preferences for antibullying interventions." *School Psychology International* 27, 475-87, http://dx.doi.org/10.1177/0143034306070435.

"Cyberbullying: A growing problem." 2010. *Science Daily*, http://www.sciencedaily.com/releases/2010/02/100222104939.htm.

Dake, J. A., Price, J. H., and Telljohann, S. K. 2003. "The nature and extent of bullying at school." *Journal of School Health* 73, 173-80, http://dx.doi.org/10.1111/j.1746-1561.2003.tb03599.x.

deLara, E., and Garbarino, J. 2003. "Words can hurt forever." *Educational Leadership* 60(6), 18-22.

DeVoe, J. F., Kaffenberger, S., and Chandler, K. 2005. "Student reports of bullying: Results from the 2001 School Crime Supplement to the National Crime Victimization Survey." Washington, DC: National Center for Education Statistics, US Department of Education.

Dijkstra, J. K., Lindenberg, S., and Veenstra, R. 2008. "Beyond the class norm: Bullying behavior of popular adolescents and its relation to peer acceptance and rejection." *Journal of Abnormal Child Psychology* 36, 1289-99, http://dx.doi.org/10.1007/s10802-008-9251-7.

Dimmitt, C., Carey, J. C., and Hatch, T. 2007. *Evidence-Based School Counseling: Making a Difference with Data-Driven Practices.* Thousand Oaks, CA: Corwin Press.

Drago-Severson, E. 2007. "Helping teachers learn: Principals as professional development leaders." *Teachers College Record* 109, 70-125.

Dweck, C. S., and Leggett, E. L. 1988. "A social-cognitive approach to motivation and personality." *Psychological Review* 95, 256-73, http://dx.doi.org/10.1037//0033-295X.95.2.256.

Earhart, M. 2005. "Bullying: What's being done and why schools aren't doing more." *Journal of Juvenile Law* 25, 26-36.

Einarsen, S., Hoel, H., Zapf, D., and Cooper, C., eds. 2003. *Bullying and Emotional Abuse in the Workplace: International Perspectives in Research and Practice.* New York, NY: Taylor and Francis.

Eliot, M., Cornell, D., Gregory, A., and Fan, X. 2010. "Supportive school climate and student willingness to seek help for bullying and threats of violence." *Journal of School Psychology* 48, 533-53, http://dx.doi.org/10.1016/j.jsp.2010.07.001.

Epstein, M., et al. 2008. "Reducing behavior problems in the elementary classroom: A practice guide" (NCEE 2008-012). Washington, D.C.: National Center for Education Evaluation and Regional Assistance, US Department of Education.

Espelage, D. L., and Swearer, S. M. 2003. "Research on school bullying and victimization: What have we learned and where do we go from here?" *School Psychology Review* 32, 365-83.

Espelage, D. L., and Swearer, S. M., eds.. 2011. *Bullying in North American schools*. New York: Taylor and Francis.

Feinberg, T. 2003. "Bullying prevention and intervention." *Principal Leadership* 4(1), 10-14.

Field, E. M. 2007. *Bully Blocking: Six Secrets to Help Children Deal with Teasing and Bullying.* Philadelphia: Jessica Kingsley.

Fight Crime: Invest In Kids. 2003. Bullying prevention is crime prevention,   http://www.fightcrime.org/state/usa/reports/bullying-prevention-crime-prevention-2003.

Fitzpatrick, K. M., Dulin, A. J., and Piko, B. F. 2007. "Not just pushing and shoving: School bullying among African American adolescents." *Journal of School Health* 77, 16-22, doi:10.1111/j.1746-1561.2007.00157.

Freiberg, H. J., Huzinec, C. A., and Templeton, S. M. 2009. "Classroom management—a pathway to student achievement: A study of fourteen inner-city elementary schools." *The Elementary School Journal* 110, 63-80, http://dx.doi.org/10.1086/598843.

Frisén, A., Jonsson, A., and Persson, C. 2007. "Adolescents' perception of bullying: Who is the victim? Who is the bully? What can be done to stop bullying?" *Adolescence* 42, 749-61.

Garandeau, C. F., and Cillessen, A. H. N. 2006. "From indirect aggression to invisible aggression: A conceptual view on bullying and peer group manipulation." *Aggression and Violent Behavior* 11, 612-625, http://dx.doi.org/10.1016/j.avb.2005.08.005.

Gastic, B. 2008. "School truancy and the disciplinary problems of bullying victims." *Educational Review* 60, 391-404, http://dx.doi.org/10.1080/00131910802393423.

Gastic, B., and Gasiewski, J. A. 2008. "School safety under NCLB's unsafe school choice option." Perspectives on Urban Education, 5(2), http://www .urbanedjournal.org/archive/volume-5-issue-2-spring-2008.

Gifford-Smith, M. E., and Brownell, C. A. 2003. "Childhood peer relationships: Social acceptance, friendships, and peer networks." *Journal of School Psychology* 41, 235-84, http:/dx.doi.org/10.1016/S0022-4405(03)00048-7.

Greene, M. B. 2006. "Bullying in schools: A plea for measure of human rights." *Journal of Social Issues* 62, 63-79, http://dx.doi.org/10.1111/j.1540-4560.2006.00439.x.

Guerra, N., Williams, K., and Sadek, S. 2011. "Understanding bullying and victimization during childhood and adolescence: A mixed methods study." *Child Development* 1, 295-310. doi:10.1111/j.1467-8624.2010.01556.x.

Gunning, I. 2004. "Knowing justice, knowing peace: Further reflections on justice, equality, and impartiality in settlement oriented and transformative mediations." *Journal of Conflict Revolution,* http://www.cojcr.org/vol5no2/CAC211.pdf.

Hammel, L. R. 2008. "Bouncing back after bullying: The resiliency of female victims of relational aggression." *Mid-Western Educational Researcher* 21(2), 3-14.

Harlin, R. P. 2008. "Bullying and violence issues in children's lives: Examining the issues and solutions." *Childhood Education* 84, 336-39, http://dx.doi.org/10.1080/00094056.2008.10523039.

Hellams, R. N. 2008. "A comparative analysis of principals' and teachers' perceptions of bullying in middle schools in three South Carolina school districts." PhD diss., ProQuest, UMI no. 3361392.

Hertzog, J. 2013 "The culture of bullying." National Bullying Prevention Center, http://www.pacer.org/bullying/nbpm/

Hirschstein, M. K., et al. 2007. "Walking the talk in bullying prevention: Teacher implementation variables related to initial impact of the Steps to Respect Program." *School Psychology Review* 36, 3-21.

Holmgren, J., Lamb, J., Miller, M., and Werderitch, C. 2011. "Decreasing bullying behaviors through discussing young-adult literature, role-playing activities, and establishing a school-wide definition of bullying in accordance with a common set of rules in language arts and math. Action research project. Saint Xavier University, Chicago.

Horne, A. M., Stoddard, J. L., and Bell, C. D. 2007. "Group approaches to reducing aggression and bullying in school." *Group Dynamics: Theory, Research, and Practice* 11, 262-71, http://dx.doi.org/10.1037/1089-2699.11.4.262.

Horton, P. 2011. "School bullying and power relations in Vietnam." PhD diss., WorldCat, OCLC no. 7813427421.

Hurley, C. T. 2012. "Middle school principals' responses to bullying: Comparing school bullying incidents and their perceived seriousness." PhD diss., ProQuest, UMI no. 3526432.

Hymel, S., Rocke-Henderson, N., and Bonanno, R. 2005. "Moral disagreement: A framework for understanding bullying among adolescents." In. O. Aluede, A. G. McEachern, and M. C. Kenny, eds. *Peer Victimization in Schools: An International Perspective* (pp. 1-11). New Delhi, India: Kamla-Raj Enterprises.

Jankauskiene, R., et al. 2008. "Associations between school bullying and psychosocial factors." *Social Behavior and Personality: An International Journal* 36, 145-62, http://dx.doi.org/10.2224/sbp.2008.36.2.145.

Juvonen, J. 2005 March/April. "Myths and facts about bullying in schools." *Behavioral Health Management* 25(2), 36-40.

Klomek, A. B., et al. 2007. "Bullying, depression, and suicidality in adolescents." *Journal of the American Academy of Child and Adolescent Psychiatry* 46, 40–49, http://dx.doi.org/10.1097/01.chi.0000242237.84925.18.

Kochenderfer-Ladd, B., and Pelletier, M. E. 2008. "Teachers' views and beliefs about bullying: Influences on classroom management strategies and students' coping with peer victimization." *Journal of School Psychology* 46, 431-53, http://dx.doi .org/10.1016/j.jsp.2007.07.005.

Kowalski, R., and Limber, S. 2007. "Electronic bullying among middle school students." *Journal of Adolescent Health*, 41(6, Supplement), S22-S30, http://dx.doi.org/10.1016/j.jadohealth.2007.08.017.

Kraft, E. M., and Wang, J. 2009. "Effectiveness of cyber bullying prevention strategies. A study on students' perspectives." *International Journal of Cyber-Criminology* 3, 513-35, http://www.cybercrimejournal. com/KraftwangJulyIJCC2009.pdf.

Kyriakides, L., et al. 2013. "Improving the school learning environment to reduce bullying: An experimental study." *Scandinavian Journal of Educational Research* 51(4), 1-26, http://dx.doi.org/10.1080/0 0313831.2013.773556.

Lawner, E. K., and Tersian, M. A. 2013. "What works for bullying programs." *Child Trends* 10(2), 2013-39.

Lawrence, C., and Green, K. 2005. "Perceiving classroom aggression: The influence of setting, intervention style and group perceptions." *British Journal of Educational Psychology* 75, 587-602, http://dx.doi.org/10.1348/000709905X25058.

Leff, S. S., et al. 2010. "The Preventing Relational Aggression in Schools Everyday Program: A preliminary evaluation of acceptability and impact." *School Psychology Review* 39, 569-587.

Limber, S. P. 2003. "Effects to address bullying in US schools." *American Journal of Health Education* 34(5, Supplement), S23-S29.

Limber, S. P., and Small, M. A. 2003. "State laws and policies to address bullying in schools." *School Psychology Review* 32, 445-55.

Martin, M. 2005. "The causes and nature of bullying and social exclusion in schools." *Educational Journal* 86, 28-30.

McCauley, S. A. 2007. "A comparison of student and teacher perceptions of bullying in magnet and neighborhood schools in an urban district." PhD diss., ProQuest, UMI no. 327957.

Meyer-Adams, N., and Conner, B. 2008. "School violence: Bullying behaviors and the psychosocial school environment in middle schools." *Children and Schools* 30, 211-221, http://dx.doi.org/10.1093/cs/30.4.211.

Mills, J. I. 2008. "A legislative overview of No Child Left Behind." *New Directions for Evaluation* 2008(117), 9-20, http://dx.doi.org/10.1002/ev.248.

Mishna, F., Scarcello, L., Pepler, D., and Wiener, J. 2005. "Teachers' understanding of bullying." *Canadian Journal of Education* 28, 718-38, http://dx.doi.org/10.2307 /4126452.

Mishna, F., Wiener, J., and Pepler, D. 2008. "Some of my best friends–experiences of bullying within friendships." *School Psychology International* 29, 549-73, http://dx.doi.org/10.1177/0143034308099201.

National Association for Sport and Physical Education. 2006. "Position statement: Recess for elementary school students." American Alliance for Health, Physical Education, Recreation, and Dance, http://www.aahperd .org/naspe/standards/upload/recess-for-elementary-school-students-2006.pdf.

Naylor, P., et al. 2006. "Teachers' and pupils' definitions of bullying." *British Journal of Educational Psychology* 76, 553-76, http://dx.doi.org/10.1348/000709905X52229.

Neiman, S. 2011. "Crime, violence, discipline, and safety in US public schools: 2009-10" (NCES 2011-320), http://nces.ed.gov/pubs2011/2011320.pdf.

Newman, R., and Murray, B. 2005." How students and teachers view the seriousness of peer harassment: When is it appropriate to seek help?" *Journal of Educational Psychology* 97, 347-65, http://dx.doi.org/10.1037/0022-0663.97.3.347.

Nickerson, A. B., Mele, D., and Princiotta, D. 2008. "Attachment and empathy as predictors of roles as defenders or outsiders in bullying interactions." *Journal of School Psychology* 46, 687-703, http://dx.doi.org/10.1016/j.jsp.2008.06.002.

Nix, C. L., and Hale, C. 2007. "Conflict within the structure of peer mediation: An examination of controlled confrontations in an at-risk school." *Conflict Resolution Quarterly* 24, 327-48, http://dx.doi.org/10.1002/crq.177.

Norwood, J. 2008, January. "Whole-school bullying prevention programs: The need for evidenced-based programs." Paper presented at the Proceedings of Master in Teacher Program 2006-2008 Teaching the Child in Front of You in a Changing World, The Evergreen State College, Olympia, WA.

Novick, R. M., and Isaacs, J. 2010. "Telling is compelling: The impact of student reports of bullying on teacher intervention." *Educational Psychology* 30, 283-96, http://dx.doi.org/10.1080/01443410903573123.

Obermann, M.-L. 2013. "Temporal aspects of moral disengagement in school bullying: Crystallization or escalation?" *Journal of School Violence* 12, 193-210, http://dx.doi.org/10.1080/15388220.2013.766133.

Odden, A. R., and Picus, L. O. 2008. *School Finance: A Policy Perceptive.* 4th ed. New York: McGraw-Hill.

O'Farrell, E. M. 2010. "The effects of participation of school children as mediators in contrast to non-mediators in a mentored mediation program as related to academic achievement, developmental disposition, and conflict orientation." PhD diss., ProQuest, UMI no. 3424360.

Olthof, T., et al. 2011. "Bullying as strategic behavior: Relations with desired and acquired dominance in the peer group." *Journal of School Psychology* 49, 339-59, http://dx.doi.org/10 .1016/j.jsp.2011.03.003.

Olweus, D. 1993. *Bullying at School: What We Know and What We Can Do.* Hoboken, NJ: Wiley-Blackwell.

Olweus, D. 1996a. "Bullying at school: Knowledge base and an effective intervention program." *Annals of the New York Academy of Sciences* 794, 265-76.

Olweus, D. 1996b. "Searchable inventory of instruments assessing violent behavior and related constructs in children and adolescents: The revised Bully/Victim Questionnaire." Rutgers University Behavioral Health Care, http://vinst.umdnj.edu/VAID/TestReport. asp?Code=ROBVQ.

Olweus, D. 2003, March. "A profile of bullying at school." *Educational Leadership* 60(6), 12-17.

Penuel, W. R., et al. "What makes professional development effective? Strategies that foster curriculum implementation."

American Educational Research Journal 44, 921-58, http://dx.doi.org/10.3102/0002831207308221.

Peterson, R. L., and Skiba, R. 2001. "Creating school climates that prevent school violence." *The Clearing House* 74, 155-63, http://dx.doi.org/10.1080/00098650109599183.

Pintado, I. 2006. "Perceptions of school climate and bullying in middle schools." PhD diss., University of Florida Scholar Commons, http://scholarcommons.usf.edu/cgi/viewcontent. .cgi?article=3658andcontext=etd.

Pornari, C. D., and Wood, J. 2010. "Peer and cyber aggression in secondary school students: The role of moral disengagement, hostile attribution bias, and outcome expectancies." *Aggressive Behavior* 36, 81-94, http://dx.doi.org/10.1002/ab.20336.

Powell, M. 2007. "Fort play children recreate recess." *Montessori Life: A Publication of the American Montessori Society*,19(3), 20-30.

Putallaz, M., et al. 2007. "Overt and relational aggression and victimization: Multiple perspectives within the school setting. *Journal of School Psychology* 45, 523-47.

Ramsey, C. J. 2010. "Teachers' experiences with student bullying in five rural schools." PhD diss., ProQuest, UMI no. 3398019.

Rigby, K., and Bagshaw, D. 2003. "Prospects of adolescent students collaborating with teachers in addressing issues of bullying and conflict in schools." *Educational Psychology* 23, 535-46, http://dx.doi. org/10.1080/0144341032000123787.

Rosenthal, M 2010. "Learning to Live Together": Training early childhood educators to promote socio-emotional competence of toddlers and pre-school children. *European Early Childhood Education Research Journal* 18(3), 223-40.

Rowe, F., Stewart, D., and Patterson, C. 2007. "Promoting school connectedness through whole school approaches." *Health Education* 107, 524-42, http://dx.doi.org/10.1108/09654280710827920.

Sainio, M., Veenstra, et al. 2013. "Being bullied by same-versus other-sex peers: Does it matter for adolescent victims?" *Journal of Clinical Child and Adolescent Psychology* 44, 454-66, http://dx.doi.org/1 0.1080/15374416.2013.769172.

Salmivalli, C. 2011. "Bullying and the peer group: A review." *Aggression and Violent Behavior* 15, 112-20, http://ars.els-cdn.com/ content/image/1-s2.0-S1359178910X00027-cov150h.gif.

Santiago, M. J., Otero-López, J. M., Castro, C., and Villardefrancos, E. 2009. "Occupational stress in secondary school teachers: Examining the role of students' disruptive behavior and/or attitudes and the perceived difficulty in conflict management." *European Journal of Education and Psychology* 1, 39-50.

Sapouna, M., and Samara, M. 2008. "Bullying: Why does it happen and what can we do about it?" Unpublished paper presented at Ban Bullying at Work Day, University of Warwick, UK.

Scarpaci, R. T. 2006. "Bullying: Effective strategies for its prevention." *Kappa Delta Pi Record* 42, 170-74, http://dx.doi.org/10.1080/00228958.2006 .1051802.

Scheithauer, H., et al. 2006. "Physical, verbal, and relational forms of bullying among German students: Age trends, gender differences, and correlates." *Aggressive Behavior* 32, 261-75, http://dx.doi.org/10.1002/ab.2012.

Schiffleger, E. E. 2008. "Columbine: A lesson in pragmatism: What's being done to prevent school violence and how it can be done better." Selected Works, http://works.bepress.com/cgi/viewcontent .cgi?article=1000andcontext=erin_schiffleger.

Schulte, K. Z. 2007. "Sexually degrading name-calling of secondary male students: The extent, the effects, educator responses, and victim propensity toward violence." PhD diss., ProQuest, UMI no. 3261440.

Seals, D., and Young, J. 2003. "Bullying and victimization: Prevalence and relationship to gender, grade level, ethnicity, self-esteem, and depression." *Adolescence* 38, 735-47.

Shin, Y.2010. "Psychosocial and friendship characteristics of bully/ victim subgroups in Korean primary school children." *School Psychology International* 31 (4) 372-88.

Simonsen, B., Sugai, G., and Negron, M. 2008. "Schoolwide positive behavior supports: Primary systems and practices." *Teaching Exceptional Children* 40(6), 32-40.

Skiba, R. J., and Knestling, K. 2001. "Zero tolerance, zero evidence: An analysis of school disciplinary practice." *New Directions for Mental Health Services* 2001(92), 17-43, doi:10.1002/yd.23320019204.

Skrzypiec, G., et al. 2011. "School bullying by one or more ways: Does it matter and how do students cope" *School Psychology International* 32, 288-311, http://dx.doi.org/10.1177/0143034311402308.

Smith, D. C., and Sandhu, D. S. 2004. "Toward a positive perspective on violence prevention in schools: Building connections." *Journal of Counseling and Development* 82, 287-93, http://dx.doi. org/10.1002/j.1556-6678.2004.tb00312.x.

Smith, J. D., Cousins, J. B., and Stewart, R. 2005. "Antibullying interventions in schools: Ingredients of effective programs." *Canadian Journal of Education* 28, 739-925.

Smith, J. D., er al. 2004. "The effectiveness of whole-school antibullying programs: A synthesis of evaluation research." *School Psychology Review,*33, 547-60.

Smith, P. K. 2011. "Why interventions to reduce bullying and violence in schools may (or may not) succeed: Comments on this special section." *International Journal of Behavioral Development* 35, 419-23, http://dx.doi.org/10.1177 /0165025411407459.

Solberg, M. E., Olweus, D., and Endresen, I. M. 2007. "Bullies and victims at school: Are they the same pupils?" *British Journal of Educational Psychology*, 77, 441-64, http://dx.doi.org/10.1348/000709906X105689.

Srabstein, J. C., Berkman, B. E., and Pyntikova, E. 2008. "Antibullying legislation: A public health perspective." *Journal of Adolescent Health* 42, 11-20.

Standifer, R. L., Stark, J. B, and Wall, J. A. 2001. "Mediation: A current review and theory development." *The Journal of Conflict Resolution* 45(3), 370-91, http://ezproxylocal.library.nova.edu/login?url=http://search.proquest.com/docview/224563026?accountid=6579.

Stassen Berger, K. 2007. "Update on bullying at school: Science forgotten?" *Developmental Review* 27, 90-126, http://dx.doi.org/10.1016/j.dr.2006.08.002.

Swart, E., and Bredekamp, J. 2009. "Non-physical bullying: exploring the perspectives of Grade 5 girls." *South African Journal of Education* 29, 405-25.

Swearer, S. M., et al. 2010. "What can be done about school bullying? Linking research to educational practice." Educational Researcher 39, 38-47, http://dx.doi.org/10.3102/0013189X09357622.

Swearer, S. M., et al. 2008. "'You're so gay!'": Do different forms of bullying matter for adolescent males" *School Psychology Review* 37, 160-73.

Thomas, D. 2012, March 29. "The Illinois House voted Wednesday to strengthen the state's antibullying laws." *State Journal Register*, http://www.sj-r.com/x586831428/Illinois-house-passes-tougher-antibullying-law.

Ttofi, M., and Farrington, D. 2011. "Effectiveness of school-based programs to reduce bullying: A systematic and meta-analytic review." *Journal of Experimental Criminology* 7(1), 27-56.

Underwood, M. K. 2003. *Social Aggression Among Girls*. New York: Guilford Press.

Urbanski, J. 2007. "The relationship between school connectedness and bullying victimization in secondary students. PhD diss., ProQuest, UMI no. 3306896.

US Department of Education, Elementary and Secondary Education. 2010. "No Child Left Behind Act of 2001." http://www2.ed.gov/policy/elsec/leg/esea02/index.html.

US Department of Education, Office of Planning, Evaluation and Policy Development. 2011. "Analysis of state bullying laws and policies," http://www.ed.gov/about/offices/list/opepd/ppss/index.html.

US Department of Education, Office of Safe and Drug-Free Schools. 2004. "Safe and Drug-Free Schools and Communities Act: State grants." Washington, DC.

US Department of Health and Human Services, Office of Adolescent Health. 2013. "Bullying," http://www.hhs.gov/ash/oah/adolescent-health-topics/healthy-relationships/bullying.html.

Vieno, A., Gini, G., and Santinello, M. 2011. "Different forms of bullying and their association to smoking and drinking behavior in Italian adolescents." *Journal of School Health* 81, 393-99, http://dx.doi.org/10.1111/j.1746-1561.2011.00607.x.

Vreeman, R. C., and Carroll, A. E. 2007. "A systematic review of school-based interventions to prevent bullying." *Archives of Pediatrics and Adolescent Medicine* 161, 78-88, http://dx.doi.org/10.1001/archpedi.161.1.78

Wang, J., Nansel, R., and Iannotti, R. 2011. "Cyber bullying and traditional bullying: Differential association with depression." *Journal of Adolescent Health* 48, 415-17, doi:10.1016/j.jadohealth.2010.07.012.

Wasley, L., ed. 2005. "Taking bullying seriously: Is your child a target?," http://www.matrixparents.org/pdf/matrixpackets/Bullying.pdf.

Wheelan, S., and Kesselring, J. 2005. "Link between faculty group: Development and elementary student performance on standardized tests." *Journal of Educational Research* 98, 323-30, http://dx.doi.org/10.3200/JOER.98.6.323-330.

"White House Conference on Bullying Prevention—Obama, Duncan, Experts Weigh in 2011, March 10." The Huffington Post, http:www.huffingtonpost.com.

Whitted, K. S., and Dupper, D. R. 2005. "Best practices for preventing or reducing bullying in schools." Children and Schools 27, 167-75, http://dx.doi.org/10.1093 /cs/27.3.167.

Ybarra, K. S., Espelage, D., and Mitchell, K. J. 2007. "The co-occurrence of Internet harassment and unwanted sexual solicitation victimization and perpetration: Associations with psychological indicators." *Journal of Adolescent Health* 41, 31-41.

Ybarra, M. L., et al. 2006. Examining characteristics and associated distress related to Internet harassment, findings from the Second Youth International Survey. *Pediatric* 118, 1169-77.

ADDITIONAL RESOURCES

1. Anti Bullying Network http://antibullying.net/resources wwwlinks.htm

2. American Psychological Association **http://www.apa.org**

3. Cy**berbullying** http://www.ncpc.org/topics/cyberbullying

4. **National Bullying Prevention Center http://www.pacer. org/bullying/resources**

5. **Stop Bullying http://wwwstopbullying.gov/index.html**

6. **Substance abuse and mental health services administration https://www.samhsa.gov/tribal-ttac/ resources/bullying**

ABOUT THE AUTHOR

Dwayne Ruffin, Ed.D, M.Ed, MSA, graduated from Nova Southeastern University and received his doctorate of education in organizational leadership with a concentration in conflict management. His researched focused on An  Ethnographic Examination of Middle Grade Teachers' Perceptions of Student Physical and Relational Bullying in an Urban School.

Dr. Ruffin developed this book and Bullying Resolution Model as a means of giving voice and call to action in addressing multi-level conflicts ranging from minor inappropriateness to sever or even complex dilemmas constructively. These pages reflect the dept and variety of his experience and insights gained as an educator for more than thirty years serving the learning community in the positions of Social and Emotional Behavioral Specialist, Dean of Students, Interim Assistant Principal, Curriculum Developer, Training Manager, Chief Instructor, Teacher and Mentor.

As an educator and retired U.S. Army non-commissioned officer Dr. Ruffin learned a facilitative approach to bullying prevention, conflict management, and restorative practices. Among fellow educators, he became the " go-to guy" for resolving conflicts among students.

Dr. Dwayne Ruffin still resides in Chicago, Illinois and employed with the Public school system.

Contact the author at <u>druffin357@gmail.com</u>!

Printed in the United States
By Bookmasters